A SCHOOL SURVIVAL GUIDE

HOW TO DO YOUR BEST ON TESTS

REVISED EDITION

Sara Dulaney Gilbert

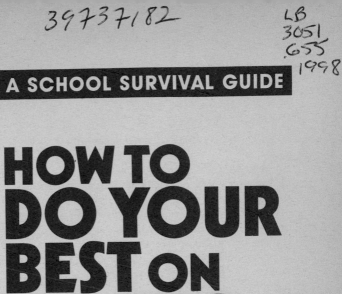

Beech Tree
New York

(Portions of this book were previously published in
How to Take Tests)

With very special thanks to Andrea

Published by Morrow Junior Books
a division of William Morrow and Company, Inc.
1350 Avenue of the Americas, New York, NY 10019
www.williammorrow.com

Printed in the United States of America.

The Library of Congress has cataloged the Morrow Junior Books version of *How to Do Your Best on Tests* as follows:
Gilbert, Sara D.
How to do your best on tests / Sara Dulaney Gilbert.—Rev. ed.
p. cm.
Rev. ed. of: How to take tests. 1983.
Summary: Discusses effective ways to successfully study for and take tests, including quizzes, final exams, and standardized tests, emphasizing the methods of preview, view, review.
ISBN 0-688-16089-1
1. Examinations—Study guides—Juvenile literature.
2. Educational tests and measurements—Study guides—Juvenile literature. 3. Test-taking skills—Juvenile literature.
[1. Examinations—Study guides. 2. Study skills.] I. Gilbert, Sara D.
How to take tests. II. Title. LB3051.G514 1998 371.26—dc21 98-14297 CIP /

Revised Beech Tree Edition, 1998
ISBN 0-688-16090-5

6 7 8 9 10

CONTENTS

I. Testing! Testing!

1. Why? 7

2. Vocabulary Prep 12

3. Getting Testwise 16

II. The Three-Step System for Testing Success

4. How It Works on Every Test 25

5. How It Works on Studying 31

6. The Testwise Way to Take a Test 42

III. Tests to Test

7. Real Tests to Try Out 73

8. The Real *Big* Tests—Standardized Tests 91

9. Where to Find More Tests 115

10. Is It Over Yet? 119

Index 125

Testing! Testing!

CHAPTER 1

WHY?

SINCE YOU HAVE OPENED THIS book, you probably

1. are beginning to realize how much tests really count, or
2. feel a bit nervous about taking tests, or
3. both of the above.

Whether you like it or not, tests are a fact of life. In fact, as your parents and your teachers may be forever reminding you, you are at a stage when tests are one of the most important facts of life that you have to face.

Why are tests important? It may be easy to understand the "why" of those big, standardized tests—they can get you into special programs, competitive high schools, or college. But it's important to do your best on classroom tests, too, because even little quizzes can have a big effect on you:

- Quizzes and bigger in-class tests are, ideally, a way for a teacher to check on your progress in a given course. If you consistently do poorly on these tests, it may mean that, for some reason, you are not learning what the course is teaching. If a whole class does poorly, a good teacher will take that as a hint to change teaching methods.
- Classroom tests can let *you* know how you're doing. If you get a low grade on a couple of quizzes, for instance, even though you've been paying attention and you've been studying, it's a sign you may not understand the course work, or you may not be studying properly. Or it may mean your style and the teacher's style don't fit! Whatever the reason, you're better off knowing early that you have to shape up. Otherwise, you'll be in trouble when the "big tests" come around.
- "Little" tests can be an easy way to establish a good image. Whether they admit it or not, whether they even realize it or not, teachers

often form an impression of the performance levels of individual students and may judge students' work accordingly as the school year goes on. So if you take the early quizzes and small tests seriously, you may create a situation in which the teacher, seeing your name on a more important test paper, will assume you will do well and grade accordingly. Is this fair? Probably not. But it's something to keep in mind.

• Classroom tests do heavily determine students' grades for the course. Class participation, homework, and work on special projects should always be a part of your grade, of course, and more and more schools are using a "portfolio" system, which involves making a formal collection of a student's work for long-term evaluation. Still, tests are a fairly clear-cut way to rate performance. Usually teachers will count tests as about one-third of the final grade, with quizzes counting for less than larger exams. By your grades, of course, you pass or fail. So in a very real way tests *can* set the direction for your life. Your grades can determine what type of class or school you qualify for in middle or high school. That, in turn, can influence the next steps that you can take after you leave school.

Equally important, those grades go into your permanent record, and that permanent record makes up a portrait of you—the most significant one that an employer or an advanced-education admissions officer will ever see.

• Standardized aptitude and achievement tests add even more detail to that portrait. Rightly or wrongly, they tell important people in your present and future what you can or can't be, should or shouldn't do: who you are or who you will be.

Knowing more now about the "why" of tests, it should be easy to see the "why" of getting all the help you can with test taking. And that's what you'll find in this book: experts' advice, as well as resources for even more help—whether in the library, by mail, or on the Web.

This book will probably not help you enjoy tests or look forward to them. Nor can it guarantee that every test you take will be an easy A. But the studying and test-taking techniques that you learn here will help you to approach tests in ways that will probably improve your grades.

Here's a preview of what you'll find in this book:

How to get testwise—that begins in the next chapter.

What you'll find on various types of tests—
that's in sections II and III.
When you'll face which tests and
Where you can find practice tests—that's in
section III.

As you get into it, *How to Do Your Best on Tests* also helps you get the most important test-taking help you can: practice! Throughout the book, you'll get a good view of test samples and self-tests to work with—plus need-to-know boxes to help you focus on key how-to's. Then, at the end, you'll find a special way to review and lock in all you've learned about how to do your best on tests.

CHAPTER 2

VOCABULARY PREP

PREVIEW . . . VIEW . . . REVIEW . . . that's how you succeed best in taking tests. What do these words mean? Well, since vocabulary is an important part of many tests, let's start by taking a look at how to figure out *these* vocabulary words.

The way to figure out anything, from a word to a whole test, is to break it into sections, start with the sections we *do* know, and then figure out the rest from there.

Start with the part you're most likely to know: *View* means "to look at or to consider" and *pre-* is a prefix (or the beginning piece of a word) meaning "before," so *preview* means to look at before, or ahead of, taking an action.

Re- is a prefix meaning "again," so *review* means to look at or consider *again*.

Preview . . . view . . . review is also the best way to study, and to read a book. Try it right now:

Preview *this* book: go through it all. Look through the table of contents—that's an outline of the whole book. Look at the highlighted boxes and text. Look over the self tests and test samples.

You'll see that the book is organized by this system, too: a preview that tells you what you are going to learn . . . a view of what you want to learn . . . and a review to help you go over what you've learned.

Previewing like this gets your brain ready to take in all the information you need to know.

"Testwise" is an important word to add to your vocabulary. It means, not smart or better, but simply "wise about tests."

Testwise people are at their best on tests because they understand that there are really only a few types of tests. No matter how fancy the format, the contents are always made up of one or more of the following: multiple choice, true-false, fill in the blanks, matching, essay, or computation.

A NEED-TO-KNOW TEST ABOUT TESTS

What do *you* know about tests? Here's a need-to-know quiz to check it out:

A **multiple choice** test is one that
- (a) always has many right answers.
- (b) never has more than one right answer.
- (c) offers several answers to choose from.
- (d) you can do quickly.

True-false tests give you only two choices: T____ F____

A **fill-in-the-blanks** test asks you to fill in a space with your own _____. Or with a _____ chosen from a list:
- (a) buffalo (b) word (c) diagram (d) encyclopedia

Matching tests ask you to connect related definitions or concepts with one another—like the test on page 74.

Essay means literally "to try." In the context of testing, it means to write a long or short composition in response to a test question, displaying your knowledge of the subject. For instance, answer this: Are essay questions more or less difficult than short-answer questions? _____ Why or why not? _____

Comprehension tests call for either an essay or for short answers to questions based on reading material provided within the test. For instance, read the first paragraph on page 12, then list three steps that testwise people take to succeed at a test: (a) _____ (b) _____ (c) _____

Computation: Any test that asks mathematical questions, or asks you to do figuring with _____.

These are important words to add to your testing vocabulary, too, because each one signals a special approach to the form you face on your test paper.

And a testwise person knows what approach to take to each. You can, too—keep reading!

CHAPTER 3

GETTING TESTWISE

TESTWISE STUDENTS TEND TO USE all the test-taking techniques they can, including the preview . . . view . . . review approach. They may come by these skills naturally, or through common sense, or by making a focused effort to learn them.

A few schools include study skills and test-taking techniques as part of their programs, but too often students are simply told that they will "have an exam next week." And that serves only to scare, provoking such responses as "What do I do about that?" "How can I stuff that information into my head?"

"What will happen to me if I don't get a good grade?"

Sometimes teachers scare students on purpose, to get them to take the test seriously. Parents, perhaps without meaning to, may scare kids by putting a lot of pressure on them to do well. Some kids have had bad test-taking experiences in the past, and this affects their current feeling about tests.

Testwise students get scared, too, but they find ways of dealing with or working through their fears. Those techniques can be learned, too.

The testwise members of your class are not necessarily the brightest ones. They may not even be the hardest workers. But they know how to study and prepare. They also have a positive attitude, as well as a relaxed approach that comes from knowing how to take tests. They know that doing their best is important, but that tests aren't *the* most important thing in life. They don't have to waste time or energy over that kind of worry or sweat over the specific techniques demanded by each type of test question.

The naturally testwise among your classmates don't have to be the only ones who do well on exams, because it is really not so hard to learn how to do your best on tests.

You can become testwise. How? By doing what the testwise do—they know that the following elements are just as important as knowledge of the material being tested:

Listening: They listen in class ahead of time, and they listen carefully to the instructions at the start of the test.

Attitude: An attitude that conveys the sense that they take this class and this test seriously, and a positive attitude that they will do well. Sometimes this is just a put-on, but it works anyway!

Instructions: Instructions are the *most* important part of *any* test, and they must be understood thoroughly.

Calm: Remaining calm is the key to testwise strategy. Even when they don't feel calm, they know how to settle their nerves and put their fears aside.

Questions: Questions are always smart. The testwise are never afraid to ask any question about any part of any test at any time.

Feedback: After a test, getting feedback matters. It helps people keep learning and do better on the next test—and it also creates a good impression.

Successful test taking is not just a matter of how much you know. It is a skill in itself, and one that you can learn.

Start now.

Review what you've read in this chapter so far, then get out a pencil and a piece of paper and take this testwise quiz.

Read *all* of these questions before answering any of them. *Answer* by circling the correct letter, or letters.

1. The best way to take a test is to
   - (a) study.
   - (b) preview first.
   - (c) be careful.
   - (d) not panic.
   - (e) all of the above.

2. Test taking is
   - (a) hard.
   - (b) a skill in itself.
   - (c) easy when you know how.
   - (d) something that takes practice.
   - (e) all of the above.

3. You can do poorly on a test if
   (a) you haven't studied.
   (b) you are scared.
   (c) you've done poorly before.
   (d) you don't know the answers.
   (e) all of the above.

4. This book will
   (a) not give you all the answers.
   (b) help develop your study skills.
   (c) help you feel better about tests.
   (d) share secrets of testwise students.
   (e) all of the above.

5. Do not answer any of the above questions. Answer only this item. You have now learned that
   (a) you don't follow instructions as well as you thought you did.
   (b) you do follow instructions well.
   (c) sometimes all the answers on a multiple-choice test are "correct."
   (d) instructions are a crucial part of any test.
   (e) none of the above.

Testwise students would know to preview by reading the instructions, then to view *all* the questions, so they would answer *only* question #5.

How'd *you* do? If you think you need more testwise "tricks," you'll find them in the next section.

NEED-TO-KNOW QUESTIONS TO ASK

The most important thing that you can do to succeed at taking tests is to ask questions about anything you need to understand—questions from the first day of class to the middle of the big test, and even questions about what it is you need to ask questions about. Whether you are preparing for a quiz or for a standardized test:

- Find out as much as you can, as far in advance as possible.
- Ask about the grading or scoring system, because this will affect how you allocate your time.
- Keep clear about course material as it's being taught— the real "trick" to test success is to keep up with the class work.

Here are the kinds of questions a student needs to ask about (almost) every test—way in advance of the test, when the test is being given, or both:

- Why is this test being given?
- What does the test giver want to get from it?
- What kind of test is it?
- What is the best way to work it? For example, is guessing OK?
- Does speed count?
- Are there points for part-right answers?
- How is the test graded?
- Where will the test be given?
- When will the test be given?
- Is there a schedule of regular exams?
- How long will the test take?

The Three-Step System for Testing Success

CHAPTER 4

HOW IT WORKS ON EVERY TEST

THERE'S NO SECRET, REALLY, TO being testwise.

The most effective way to take tests successfully—and to study and do homework—say the experts, is to preview . . . view . . . review.

> **preview:** to look over all the material first
> **view:** then to work at it
> **review:** to go back through it all again when you are finished

This simple three-step process allows anyone to succeed at testing. Once you get into the habit of *studying* this way, you'll probably find that you will remember more, so that even a surprise quiz won't rattle you.

Why does this three-step system help? Because it works the way your brain works. When you preview first, you become aware of the hard items, and your brain has time to work on them. You will find that questions that seemed impossible at first are a lot easier when you review and go back over them.

This pattern proves efficient in practical terms, too. It helps you to know ahead of time what you need to do, allows you to do it, and permits time afterward to make sure you did what you intended.

Here's how it works on any test.

PREVIEW

Too often, when students face a test paper, they feel such pressure from the time limit or from their shaky grasp of the required information that they immediately plunge into the first problem or question without reading through the directions or giving any thought to the overall test. Testwise students, however, know that if they invest a certain amount of effort and time in previewing the test—about one-tenth the total time allowed for the test—they will be rewarded.

Before you start working on the test, read or listen to the instructions carefully:

- Did the teacher say to write, for instance, on *every other* line?
- Are you supposed to put your name in the right-hand or the left-hand corner? Last name first or first name first?
- Should you underline, circle, or X out the *right* answer in a multiple choice list? Or the *wrong* answers?
- Is there a time limit?
- Will extra points be lost for errors, or is it safe to guess at answers?
- Do you use pen or pencil?
- If your teacher is reading the test questions, are you supposed to write down the questions as well as the answers, or only the answers?
- Can you work on the entire test in whatever order you choose, or must you go section by section?

Often students are so eager to begin the test or to get it over with that they don't pay proper attention to the instructions. Or they may find the teacher's instructions irritating or silly, so they simply ignore them. Most classroom teachers have reasons for requiring precision in following instructions. Either they have designed the quiz or test to be graded according to a specific pattern; or they are trying to help their students learn to follow instructions to the letter in order to prepare them for standardized tests, which are scored electronically and give no leeway for incorrectly followed instructions. No matter what the test, remember that the instructions are a very important part of it.

Quickly read through the entire test (or as much of it as you are allowed to see at one time). As you skim it, make a note, either mentally or jotted on scrap paper, about which questions or sections

- seem easiest or hardest
- count for the most and the least
- you don't, at first glance, understand completely.

By doing that, even for a short quiz, you will

- gain an important overall picture of what the test is about
- start working in advance, at least in the back of your mind, on the more puzzling items.

VIEW
When it comes time to actually *do* the test, which questions should you answer first? Unless other-

wise instructed, always start with the easiest. Next go to the ones that count for the most. If there are essay questions, write a neat outline of a good answer to each. Finally, go back to the harder questions and to items you had skipped.

REVIEW

First thing to review: the instructions. Have you followed all directions *exactly*? You might answer an entire section wrong if you have not read the instructions properly. You can lose out completely if your answers are not in the right form.

Then, check the answers you've put down. Be sure they are easy to read.

When you're as satisfied as you can be with what you've done, go over any questions you haven't done and see if you can put your best guess down—unless this test is scored so that no answer punishes you less than an incorrect answer (see page 79).

As you can see, none of these techniques has anything to do with the knowledge that exams are supposed to test, yet each of them is vital to scoring well.

You'll find tests to practice your new skills on in chapters 7 and 8.

The three-step preview . . . view . . . review system works in studying, too, as you'll find out in the next chapter. Wait! Before you decide to *skip* the next chapter because you want to focus only on test success, think about this: By using the three-step system on studying and homework, you increase your chances of test success with no sweat or cramming.

MATCH UP WHAT YOU KNOW ABOUT THE THREE-STEP SYSTEM

This quiz shows how the three-step system applies to every study and test situation. For each of the following, answer whether the activity is a *preview,* a *view,* or a *review.*

1. Noting test dates in your calendar _____
2. Reading the homework questions *before* you read the assignment _____
3. Re-checking each arithmetic problem before handing in a test _____
4. Asking the meaning of a word in an essay test question _____
5. Going over a test grade with the teacher _____
6. Doing the easiest questions first _____

[Answers: 1. preview; 2. preview; 3. review; 4. preview; 5. review; 6. view] Are you getting testwise?

CHAPTER 5

HOW IT WORKS ON STUDYING

PREVIEW . . . VIEW . . . REVIEW. THIS three-step system is helpful for taking all types of tests—from classroom quizzes to standardized tests. The same system applies to another step in preparing for exams: studying for them.

Some students do well on exams without ever seeming to study; others study all the time without doing so well. Why? The answer has less to do with relative intelligence than with the ability to study in the right way.

You will do better on tests if you know *how* to study.

That may sound like a very obvious statement, but you might be surprised at how few students know how to study effectively. In fact, it's a good bet that, no matter how well you think you do, you will have picked up at least a few new tips by the time you finish this chapter.

Although the ability to study is vital to learning and to doing well in school, and although experts know a great deal about how people learn, study skills are rarely taught in schools at any level.

"Study" is one of those words that tends to make people clutch. A better word than "study" is "review." When you study material, you want to preview it and then view it again and again from many angles. Review your notes right after every class and add a preview and review to your homework every night. Do this every day, and you'll be preparing effectively for a final from the first day of class.

Does that sound like a lot of work? It may, but in the long run you make your school life much simpler with that three-step approach, especially when you get familiar with how *you* best study.

WHAT IS YOUR STUDY STYLE?

We all have our own strengths and weaknesses—perhaps especially when it comes to school. Some students take to languages naturally but don't even try to make an effort at math, because they "can't do it." You may feel that you are terrible at science, though English is a snap. A negative attitude can easily defeat you, so it's important to get a handle on it.

Why do you feel good at some subjects and rotten at others? Did you have a math teacher once who didn't like you or didn't teach in a way that you understood? Or did you always like science in elementary school because of the teacher or the class? Maybe a parent is in the habit of saying "I was always great in . . ." and you imagine that you have to follow along. If you're going to do well in the subjects you "can't do," you may have to wipe the slate clean and start out fresh with a better frame of mind.

You might find it useful to learn whether your judgment of your abilities is correct. Talk with your teachers, or ask a parent to do it, to find out what your test scores say about your skills. You may well be stronger in some areas than in others, and if so, you can get help for your weak points from a teacher, tutor, or possibly even a classmate. That's a lot better than simply expecting to fail, because when you expect to fail, you are likely to do so.

Now take a close look at your personal study habits. Do you always find it easy to put off until tomorrow anything you don't feel like doing today? Then you will need to get tough with yourself about sticking to your study schedule. Always do your homework before doing anything else, and then reward yourself somehow for being good.

Do you know that you "ought" to do well, but you aren't quite sure why? Maybe you need to think about goals. What are some of your dreams? Is there a special school or special program you'd like to get into? How could doing your best on tests help you get there? If you keep a goal like that in mind, working hard will be easier. Or you might make a bet with a friend or family member about what grades you'll get, so your goal would be to win the bet.

Are you the kind of person who's used to having things come fast and easily? That might make you give up too soon when the work is more difficult, so do the hard stuff first.

Are you more interested in getting a task done quickly, no matter what the quality? Then practice telling yourself that the work isn't done until you've gone back and checked it at least once.

Are you a perfectionist, who may be overly critical of the quality of your work? If so, you may try to do much more than is necessary and thus spread your efforts too thin. Or you may take so long to "get it just right" that you never get an assignment done. Try to set time limits within which you must finish your work, no matter what.

Finally, what kind of learner are you? We all have our own learning styles. Some people learn well through their ears, some through their eyes, and some through their hands or entire bodies. To get an idea of your own style, ask yourself this: If you wanted to learn the words to a new hit song, could you do it simply by listening to the lyrics a few times on the radio? Would you write down the words as you heard them and then memorize them from the paper? Or would you have to play the song on an instrument or sing along a lot to get the words down?

Could you learn a new swimming stroke just by listening to someone describe it? Could you watch a swimmer doing it and then do it yourself? Or would you need to get into the pool and actually practice before you could get it right?

Think about your answers, because they will indicate what study techniques are best for you. If you learn by hearing, for instance, you may find it especially useful to read your notes or text aloud when you're studying—or even use a tape recorder. If you're a *sight* learner, you'll want to take complete notes and spend a lot of time reading and studying the charts and illustrations in your books. If you learn physically, you'll do well to "push" your notes around by making charts and diagrams, doing all the practice sections in your text, and maybe even acting out your material.

If you understand your personal learning style, you'll see why you're having more trouble in some classes than in others, because teachers have their own styles, too. If you're a *visual* learner with a *verbal* teacher, you'll learn the material better if you work at making visual interpretations of the teacher's words. You'll need to review according to your own style.

DO YOU NEED A NEW STUDY ATTITUDE?

To study effectively, you have to *want* to do well. The words "study" and "student" come from an old Latin word meaning "eager." You may be eager, at least in some of your courses, to learn just for the sake of absorbing knowledge. You may be eager for good grades and test scores at this level of your education, so that you have a chance to choose from among the best schools when you reach the next level.

Whatever your personal motivation for success, you do need to have a positive attitude. You might not feel exactly eager, but you should want to learn and use good study and test-taking habits. The fact that you are reading this book is a sign of your positive attitude.

Students who have this attitude show it by attending class regularly, by paying attention, and by taking notes. They do homework assignments carefully and on time, and when they miss a class or an assignment, they make up what they missed.

Such conscientious behavior is beneficial in two ways. It guarantees that when exam time comes you will have all the material you need for study and review. It also makes a good impression on your teacher—and this is an important part of success.

So think for a moment about your attitude. Why do you want to learn how to do your best on tests? Now that you know this book isn't just a list of test-taking tricks, are you willing to put some effort into learning how to study?

Study starts with paying attention in class. During class, even if you're not required to take notes, jot down any of your own ideas that the teacher's discussion may trigger. When you read a chapter in a textbook, do the same thing. That kind of mental activity aids memory and helps to keep your attention from wandering.

Finally, remember to write down your assignment and any special instructions that go with it. That way you'll be sure to do it right!

As soon as possible after a class, review the notes you took during it. Studies of learning patterns show that the sooner you go over material, the better and longer you will remember it.

THE THREE-STEP APPROACH TO READING IT RIGHT

When you read to learn, study, and remember, you must do it differently from the way you read for fun. To retain information efficiently—to absorb the maximum amount in the shortest time, and hold on to it for the longest period—you preview . . . view . . . and review.

To *preview* any book or chapter that you will be reading, read through the table of contents, the chapter headings and subheadings, picture captions, charts, even the index—anything that is set apart from the text and that gives an idea of what the book is about. Read any summaries in the book. Read through any chapter questions that may be included, too, even if they aren't assigned, and go over any questions about the reading that your teacher may want you to answer.

At the *view* stage, while you read, take notes—notes about what the chapter is about, and also on what your preview has shown you're supposed to get out of it. If you're allowed to, mark the main points in the textbook. If not, jot them down in your notebook. Work the sample problems in a math or science book. Ask yourself questions as you read. Right now, for example, a question you should be asking is "Why question the book?" The answer: Because the mental action of asking and answering helps your mind hold the material better than the rather passive act of simply reading.

Make notes of items you find confusing while reading. Go back and try to figure them out for yourself, but if you can't, remind yourself to ask your teacher in the next class.

Reviewing is off to an easy start if you have been assigned questions to answer for homework. Read each question and go back through the chapter to find the complete answer. But whether or not you have such an assignment, you should review the reading. Try the following techniques to see which help you best to remember what you read:

- Reread the assignment one paragraph or section at a time. Look away from it, and summarize it out loud.
- Write down a list of questions on the topic of the chapter, then write out your answers to them.
- Make an outline of the chapter that covers the main points and all the subtopics.
- List all key words, concepts, formulas, equations, names, and dates, and fill in all the information that pertains to them.
- Note points that may be brought up in class as topics for either questions or discussions so that you will be prepared to participate.

Follow a similar procedure for an in-depth review of your day's classroom notes. Skim over them again; highlight the main points; organize them in your own fashion; recite them; ask questions (for example, "How does this tie in with what I've just read in the text assignment?").

And before you count yourself finished for the night, quickly skim the highlights of the notes and reading for that class since your last test. Fifteen minutes for each course per day will be enough to keep all the material fresh in your mind.

All this may sound like too much work, but when you do your reading according to such an effective system, you will find that you make much better use of your time than you do when you simply read. It may take one and a half times as long, but this type of review is at least *twice* as effective, so you're actually saving time and energy.

Research has shown that the brain retains material much more effectively from frequent brief reviews than from a single long one. Also, by making the effort to take notes and to recite out loud, you are taking an active role in your studies. Psychologists find that active review is much more valuable than passive reading. Therefore, you'll likely remember the material so well that you can cut down on the effort and worry of studying for bigger tests and exams.

TEST IT OUT: THE SYSTEM WORKS!

To see how well the three-step system works to help you read effectively, read the first half of this chapter using the reading tips above. Wait several hours. Have someone quiz you on the material. Did you get an A?

CHAPTER 6

THE TESTWISE WAY TO TAKE A TEST

PREVIEW . . . VIEW . . . REVIEW— that's the testwise way to take a quiz, test, or exam. The time to put the three-step system to work, though, is long *before* the test.

FIRST, STUDY

Testwise students start preparing for the final exam on the first day of class! This isn't as terrible as it sounds. All it means is that you do what previous chapters have outlined:

- Ask if there is going to be a midterm or final exam.
- Review your work every day so that it

has time to sink in gradually. This way, you won't have to cram in all the material at the last minute.

- Pay attention to the smaller classroom tests you take so that you get a feel for the teacher's approach to tests.
- Go over with the teacher any quizzes or tests you do badly on, so that you don't make the same mistakes twice.
- Ask for help with any material that causes you trouble, so that you won't get stuck the night before the exam.
- Study for the right test. This may sound silly, but it's not. Many students fail to ask their teacher what material the exam will and will not cover, so they waste their time rereading notes and texts that aren't directly related. Or they concentrate on only one portion of the course work, forgetting that a final exam will likely cover everything learned from day one. (But remember that teachers can get quite irritated if, every time your hand goes up, it signals a "Will-this-be-on-the-exam?" question. You'd be wise to wait until just before you're ready to begin your final studying to ask for details.)
- The form of the exam, too, will make a big dif-

ference in how you study, so find out if you can expect true-false questions, multiple-choice, short answers, essays, or a combination. If it will be a combination, ask which part will carry the heaviest weight.

- Organize your study time. Plan ahead, so that for a few weeks before your big exams you'll know you have the extra time to spend reviewing. Write out a schedule, or make notes on a calendar, so you won't be too tempted to avoid the situation. Allow the most time for work on your weakest courses.

Get together with friends who are also serious about doing well on exams and study jointly. You might even try to find study mates who are strong in the areas where you're weak. Go over notes and assignments to be sure you don't have any gaps. Work together to figure out points you don't understand, and quiz each other.

STUDYING THE TESTWISE WAY

You, of course, are the one responsible for your own studying. There's no need for panic, though, because all you're going to do is follow your review pattern in a more concentrated form.

- Organize your material. For example, in the previous weeks or months, you may have covered major topics A, B, C, and D. Clip together your notes, study outlines, homework papers, and quizzes for each topic, and use slips of paper to mark your text or other reading books by topic. Plan to study each topic separately. Not only does breaking the material into chunks make the job seem smaller, but your brain won't get as exhausted as it would if you plowed through the whole mass at once. You'll learn and remember more from several short sessions on specific subjects than from one long, broad one.

  You are better off starting with the *middle* sections (in this case, topics B and C) because people tend to remember beginnings and endings more readily than middles.

- Preview . . . view . . . review. For each section, glance through all the material, letting it jog your memory. (If you have been reviewing regularly all along, you may be surprised at how much you remember.) But that is not enough. Educational experts and expert test takers say that you have to *overlearn*—you have to be able to recite the material almost without thinking—if only to give yourself the important feeling of confidence that you *know* you know it.

Don't just keep rereading all your notes and assignments, though, since that will just confuse and overload you. Instead, as you go through each section, stop periodically to recite *out loud* the main points you've just covered, as much from memory as possible. After reading through all of one section, skimming the whole thing if necessary or just your highlighted notes, begin to boil it down and summarize it. Summarize in outline form, as diagrams, into a tape recorder—however you are comfortable. If you get stumped, go back to your notes; but keep at it, putting the information into your own words. What you are doing is using your eyes, ears, voice, and hands as multiple pathways to get the information into your brain. Then, once or twice a day, go through these outlines and lists and continue to recite and review them out loud whenever possible.

- Practice. Using old tests, questions from the textbook and from homework assignments, or—even better—questions that you've made up while thinking about the test work, give yourself an exam. Write the questions out and then write your answers, pulling in as many facts for each as you can. Or exchange tests with your friends for practice. When you do run through such an exam, do it under exam conditions: turn off the radio, TV, or CD player, clear your desk or table, and start with a fresh blank piece of paper. (Many people can study when slouched in a chair listening to music, but they blank out when bleaker, quieter surroundings say "TEST!") After you've finished the exam, correct it—go back over your notes and texts to check for accuracy and thoroughness.

• Prepare for the right kind of exam!

For an *essay,* make up questions that, on the basis of earlier tests and points emphasized by the teacher, you can predict are likely to be on the exam. Write out answers without referring to notes, and do it within a time limit similar to the one you will probably have on the actual test. Jot down a rough outline and fill in as much detail as you can. Memorize the outlines for the most likely essay questions. (The memorization tips and techniques on pages 50–55 should help.) And be sure you know how to spell the important words that you are likely to need.

Don't think that just because essay questions allow some room for individuality or fudging, you can get away with learning only generalities. The more relevant names, dates, places, formulas, or other facts you can squeeze into your essays, the better your answer will look. Such readily available detail is also useful if you have to finish your exam essay in outline form; and just in case you run into an essay on the test that you feel very fuzzy about, the more hard facts you have stored in your mind, the more success you'll have at changing the subject while still showing that you know *something*.

For *short-answer* questions, you will definitely need to know all those nitty-gritty facts cold, so make lists of all the necessary details and memorize and recite them, stressing those the teacher has stressed. Boil down your notes into a tight little lump so that you can concentrate on the hard core of facts and key words. Although each type of short-answer test contains clues within it to the right answer (see pages 77–79), the better you know your facts, the more quickly you will be able to answer—and on an exam, you won't want to waste time.

Since it is hard to make up short-answer tests for yourself, have someone drill you. Take turns with a classmate putting the facts in true-false or sentence-completion form. Or have someone in your family go through your lists, asking for definitions and explanations of each term until you can answer almost without thinking. Review and restudy the parts you have a hard time with.

The best way to study for *problem-solving* exams—for example, for math or science courses —is to practice, practice, practice! Once you've got a good handle on the basic information you'll need—theories, principles, and so forth—work as many problems as you can find. Rework ones from earlier quizzes, tests, and homework; work unassigned ones in the textbook; have someone make up new problems for you. Be sure that you can understand each type of problem you will be tested on so that, for instance, no matter what the numbers involved, you will be able to recognize a time and motion problem and get to work on it without giving it a second thought.

The better prepared you are for any type of test, the more confident you will be going into it.

MAKE YOUR MEMORY WORK

For some subjects, you will have to memorize specific items—formulas, equations, word spellings, or dates, for instance. But it doesn't hurt to memorize material from any subject, since the more you can put down on the exam paper, the better you will look. Also, the more material you have ready at the front of your mind, the more quickly you'll be able to get through the test.

We have two types of memory, *short term* and *long term*. Short-term memory lasts about as long as it takes to look up a phone number and dial it; long-term memory lasts indefinitely, but it often needs to be triggered. When memorizing for an exam, you need to transfer items from the short-term department into the long-term memory bank. Since most people can remember only seven or so "bits" of short-term information at a time, the first trick is, obviously, to memorize a few pieces at a time. That means spacing your cram times well, so that you can break down your work into small chunks and push it into the long term, bit by bit.

We also have a hard time memorizing material we don't understand. See which of these lists you can memorize faster:

sad	das
and	nda
pat	tpa
put	utp
yes	eys

The nonsense syllables are much harder, right? Keep this in mind the next time you consider cramming for an exam without understanding the content clearly.

Still, even when the content is clear, memorization takes much more effort than simple reading, and it can be difficult. To do it at all, you first must want to do it. That doesn't mean you'll *enjoy* the work; for this task "want" means simply that you have the determination to get it done well enough to succeed on the exam. If your mother makes you go to the store for four items, you'll probably forget at least one, since you didn't want to do it. If she bets you a dollar that you won't remember, you're more likely to get everything. You still won't enjoy the trip, but you have an incentive to lock the list into your mind.

An understanding of the material and an incentive for remembering it are two important factors in memorization—and luckily, there are many tricks and techniques that make the effort easier.

The ones that will work best for you are those that best fit your learning style. If you are a visual person, write or draw your material and force yourself to "see it" with your mind's eye. If your ears are your keenest tools, read everything aloud or listen to your own tape recordings of it. If you need to use your entire body, try dancing, tapping your fingers, or other physical techniques.

Experiment with some of the following techniques and see which are the most effective for you:

- One way to lock something into your memory is to look at it hard, read it out loud, then close your eyes and say it aloud again. Make yourself "hear" and "see" it mentally. Finally, try to force those words and images into the back of your brain. If you do it right, you can almost feel the items being lodged in your head as they move from your short-term into your long-term memory.

- Another technique you might find helpful is to make mental pictures of the material's content. Are you studying about dinosaurs? Paint a picture in your mind's eye of how they lived. Then, to recall facts about it, you can "look" at that mental picture for reminders. Or make a mental picture of important pages in your textbooks. You may find that you can actually "read" those pages while you are taking the test.

- You can also try breaking down your material into smaller chunks or reorganizing it. To memorize definitions, work on the "a" word first, then on all the words beginning with "b," then "c," and so forth. Tick off on your fingers how many "a's," "b's," "c's," and so on, you need to recall so that you keep better track of them.

- Grouping items helps, too. If you have to know the capitals of all fifty states, for instance, group them by geographical regions—New England, Northwest, and so on. Then you'll have about eight clumps to memorize rather than fifty unrelated names.

- When you need to remember large volumes of information, find key words in each paragraph or section. Memorize those, and use them to stimulate your recollection of the whole mass.

In addition to these techniques, there are many useful memory tricks that will not only ease and lock materials into your mind but also act as hooks to bring it out when needed. For instance:

- Initial words or *acronyms*. The initials of the Great Lakes spell HOMES: *H*uron, *O*ntario, *M*ichigan, *E*rie, and *S*uperior. *M*y *D*ear *A*unt *S*ally is a reminder that in math, *M*ultiplication and *D*ivision are done before *A*ddition and *S*ubtraction. The first letter of each of the short words on page 51 spell "sappy," and rearranging the order of the nonsense syllables so you can think about them as "tuned" might make them possible to remember.
- Rhymes. "In 1492 Columbus sailed the ocean blue." "I before E except after C, or when sounded as A as in neighbor or weigh."
- Rhythm and melody. Set the words to music or a beat, and the jingle will be easy to remember, even when you're dealing with complex mathematical or scientific formulas.

When you apply tricks and techniques such as these to your style and your material, you'll find that your rhymes and jingles will be easy to remember and will trigger your memory of the actual material.

However you go about it, when you've memorized a chunk of material, write it out and/or talk it into a tape recorder, referring to your notes as little as possible. You will know that you've got it down pat when you can recite it accurately without physically seeing or hearing it.

TAKE A DEEP BREATH!

And now, there's only one more preparation step to take before the exam—relax!

The tension-relieving techniques described on pages 65–68 will help ease tensions while you're studying, let you get to sleep the night before the exam, and relax you during even the biggest of big tests. Why not try some of them now? They're simple but surprisingly effective.

The study skills and test-taking techniques that you've been learning in these chapters are effective, too. They may seem like a big effort at first, but you'll soon find that they're more than worth the trouble.

You are as ready as you will ever be or can be, and now you need to concentrate your energy and attention on the test itself.

JUST IN CASE

To be honest, of course, all that relaxation and positive thinking may not do you much good if that universally feared student's nightmare comes true and, for whatever reason, you simply do not know the answers to the test questions. Readying yourself for action in case that happens to you should also be a part of your mental preparation for exam taking. So, just in case, keep this advice in mind: *Don't ever simply walk away from a test!*

Don't just walk out of the classroom or turn in a blank paper (or worse, a paper with a rude comment on it). You might know more than you thought you did; or your scratchy notes just might be better than the answers of enough of your classmates to get you a passing grade.

Most teachers, like the rest of us, are willing to give help when it is needed, and most respect honesty. So even when you feel panicky, there's no call for panic. You always have positive options.

MEETING THE TEST

But you do know how to approach that test, don't you? No matter how big or important the test or exam is, you will follow the same steps: preview . . . view . . . review. Here's how to do it.

PREVIEW

For each test or test section, preview the questions first. For instance, if you have to correct the grammar and punctuation for the following paragraph, skimming through it you will get a feel for the changes you know must be made. Then by the time you start making those corrections, you will be much better able to select the right word or punctuation mark.

Tests (1)<u>is</u> a way of rating students. (2)"<u>Hard</u> is (3)<u>how</u> a person can call a test that (4)<u>they</u> doesn't (5)<u>like</u> but if you are (6)<u>more wiser</u> you ought to be thinking (7)<u>as how</u> they could be helping you. (8)<u>Once,</u> you have learned how to take examinations, it will be easier for you to do (9)<u>good</u> on tests.

Likewise, computation or word-analogy tests are easier if you preview *all* the possible answers ahead of time.

Alison read ½ of a book and Timothy read ¾ of his book. How many books did they read altogether?

(a) ¾
(b) ⁶⁄₁₅
(c) ²⁷⁄₃₂
(d) 1⅓
(e) none of the above

Chapter:book =

(a) book:library
(b) sentence:paragraph
(c) city:universe
(d) traffic:car

And you can start your unconscious mind working on the essay section of a test while you're figuring out the easy true-false items.

You'll also do better with reading-comprehension formats if you preview the questions *before* you read the paragraph (no matter what the instructions say). Test it out for yourself on the following paragraph:

Read This Paragraph and Answer the Questions That Follow.

The ability to relax is important to any form of competition, in test taking as well as in athletics, and relaxation before an exam can be as easy as taking a deep breath. Try this now: Close your eyes, then take a deep breath and hold it for a count of ten. Slowly release the breath, and open your eyes. Or, clench every muscle in your body and hold your breath. Maintain that tightness for a count of ten, and then gradually relax and start breathing. If you've done either or both of those simple exercises correctly, you will feel a lessening of tension in your body.

Which statements do *not* agree with what the paragraph says?
(a) Relaxation exercise is only for athletes.
(b) You'll always stay relaxed if you keep your eyes closed.
(c) Deep breathing can help release tension.
(d) Clenching all your muscles can never help you relax.

Planning, even for a few seconds, is a vital part of the preview stage of test taking. When you are allotting time for each segment of the test, one factor to consider is the weight that each question or section will carry in your test score. If the instructions do not include that information, ask. Otherwise, you might end up spending half of the test time on an item that counts toward one-twentieth of your grade!

VIEW

Only after previewing the entire test are you ready actually to take the test. Many students might think that a preview wastes valuable time, but testwise students know that this preparation is worthwhile. Your understanding of the instructions and your overview of the questions will enable you to cope effectively with the exam as a whole. Here's the way that experts recommend you proceed.

- Answer the easiest questions or work the easiest problems first. This ensures that you will get at least part of the test right, and it gives the back of your mind time to chew over the hard ones a bit.
- Go back to the tougher items. Reread them and

think about them from as many angles as possible, trying to relate them to something similar you've done in class or for homework.

- *Brainstorm.* Rather than think, I can't do it, open your head and let all your ideas flood out.
- Look for clues within the question itself. For example, in the reading-comprehension paragraph on page 58, three answers contain absolutes like "only," "always," and "never." This makes it likely that those were not included in the paragraph, and so are the right answers for the question. (You *did* read the instructions properly, didn't you?)
- If you have any questions about the items on your quiz, test, or exam, and you haven't yet asked them, do so now.
- Remember your time allotments and don't wrestle too long with any one item. If you've looked for clues, if you've racked your brain, if you've tried to get help from the test giver and still can't come up with an answer that seems comfortably right, write the item off. But if the form of the test allows it, try to put *something* down on the paper to show that you did make an effort: part of the calculations for a math problem; a few dates for a history question; some of your

thoughts about why an item might be either true or false; the outline for an essay. You may at least get some credit for showing that you tried.

REVIEW

Like previewing, reviewing is an important stage that many students must force themselves to learn. No matter how confident—or shaky—they feel about their answers on a quiz or test, testwise students know that they can never lose, and can often gain, by going over the test paper.

- Before you turn it in, check to make sure that you have put down what you had intended. Are your answers clearly marked or written? If your "7" looks like a "9," you won't get credit. Have you circled both "A" and "B"? That answer is no good. If you've marked the wrong answer line throughout a standardized test, you will come up with a negative score.
- Is your writing readable? If the test giver can't read your answers, you won't get credit.

Unless the instructions say otherwise, it's a good idea to use all the time allowed: there's always room for improvement—besides, sitting through a test makes a good impression on teachers.

HOW THE TESTWISE PSYCH UP AND COOL DOWN

What was that? Something about a testwise student feeling shaky? Sure—everybody gets nervous. But there are plenty of ways to get calm.

Even when we try to deny that we are nervous, our bodies often give us away with physical symptoms. This is because our bodies, minds, and emotions are connected parts of a single package, and because we humans are, physically, animals. The bodies of all animals ready them to fight or take flight when they are threatened or frightened. A feeling of danger—even danger from an innocent-looking paper and pencil—may make our bodies react as if they were preparing for actual combat or escape.

Fine. Nervousness, even in its severe form, is natural. The problem arises when the fear itself becomes defeating. Nerves can make it hard for you to prepare for a test, since they can hamper your mind's ability to absorb study material. A fear of tests can result in a poor performance, even when you have studied thoroughly.

Luckily, you have many ways of getting rid of that fear.

If you are afraid of tests, do you know why? Think for a moment about exams you have taken and the reactions of your parents, teachers, and friends to your test results. Think about ideas your family may have passed on to you. Try to remember ways in which significant teachers in your life have prepared you for important tests. Did they make you feel confident? Or uptight?

Those recollections can be important clues to your attitude—and a positive attitude is one of the most important factors in effective studying and successful test taking. When you are plowing through a chapter you're likely to be tested on, do you think things like I'll never be able to understand this!? This idea itself can defeat you, so focus your attention instead on completing the task, step by step.

Do you tend to remember all the times you've done badly—scored low on a test or messed up in class? Then do this: Go back over your grades and get an accurate picture of them. A "B" is not as good as an "A," but it's still a fine grade. A "C" is not so hot, until you remember how hard you tried to grasp the material in the first place. If you got marks that were nothing to be proud of at all, analyze why you did badly and think about what you would do now to do better. Did you simply not study? Well, now you will. Did you have trouble getting along with the teacher? To solve problems like that, try turning on a little charm. Did you really not understand the material? Next time you'll know to ask for extra help. The point is: Rather than dwell on the failures, think about positive ways to avoid them in the future.

You are taking steps to improve your study skills and test scores right now, so pat yourself on the back for that and for your other successes. You'll start thinking better of yourself and expecting good results. Then, through a process called the self-fulfilling prophecy, you will accomplish what you prophesy, or predict, you will. In other words, you do as well as you expect. Expect to do well—and you are more likely to.

Still, tests can feel threatening. So here are some testwise tips for keeping cool.

Are tests a headache to you? Then your head may actually ache. Do you feel that too much responsibility rests on your shoulders, wish that the teacher would get off your back, or worry that your parents will have your neck if you don't do well? Then you may well feel special tension in those parts of your body. And you may not be speaking figuratively when you say that tests make you sick to your stomach.

Remember that your mind and your body are one. Your physical well-being can be affected by your psychological attitude, and your mental state can be improved through physical means. By working to make your muscles loose and relaxed, for instance, you can ease the tension and anxiety that you feel in the pit of your stomach. Taking long walks or playing an occasional vigorous game of ball can help you unwind. Warm baths or showers help you loosen up, too.

For more thorough relaxation before you begin to study or if you can't sleep the night before a big test, try this. Sit in a comfortable chair (or lie in bed if you're ready to go to sleep). Close your eyes and take a deep breath. Then, starting with your toes, slowly make every part of your body go limp. Imagine that your arms, legs, torso, and neck are like floppy rubber bands. Don't move to your leg muscles until your feet and toes are completely loose. Work your way up the rest of your body, loosening up each joint and muscle. Your face and head are especially important to loosen up. Let your jaw sag and feel your tongue loosen. Make sure that your eyes are shut gently, not squeezed together. Feel your scalp loosen under your hair. Don't move for a while—just savor the delicious feeling of being limp and unwound.

While you're studying or taking the test, tension may creep up on you without your realizing it, both because physically you're locked in one position and because psychologically you may be fretting. It's important to stretch the tension out periodically.

- You can work the tension out of your neck and upper back by slowly rotating your head first in one direction and then in the other. Rotate your shoulders, too, and feel the kinks come out. Rub your shoulder and neck muscles firmly with your fingers, and you can feel knotted muscles untie themselves.

- You can relax your spine by alternately curving and arching it. Sitting in your chair—or, when you can, lying on your back or kneeling on all fours—curve your back into as much of a circle as you can, by sucking in your gut and pushing your chin onto your chest. Do this very slowly, and then, just as slowly, go the other way, until your belly is out, your chin is up, and your spine is a curving arch.

- To loosen your whole body and get your circulation going, swing your arms in an S-shaped motion and your legs and torso around in huge, loose circles. Stretch your head and arms up tall and tight, then let yourself droop, with your head hanging limp. Repeat this several times, inhaling deeply as you stretch up and exhaling as you sag down.

You can and should do miniversions of those stretches before and during an exam, and you can even do a form of the following total relaxer while you're sitting in the testing room:

- Tense every muscle in your body as tightly as you can and hold for a count of ten. Then, one by one, relax those muscles. Concentrate on breathing regularly and deeply. Close your eyes and listen to your breathing.
- Or close your eyes and concentrate on creating a visual image of something soothing—a meadow scene, perhaps, with butterflies, or a dark velvet curtain with a single feather float-

ing down in front of it. Focus on feeling how peaceful the vision is, and you will soon feel peaceful and relaxed yourself.

A little bit of tension is probably useful when you face a test, but it should be a positive feeling—excitement rather than anxiety, a slightly keyed-up feeling that comes from wanting to do well rather than fearing doing badly. Think of the difference between the excitement you feel while watching your favorite sports team play or watching an adventure movie, versus the nervousness you'd experience if you were actually on the field or in the middle of that dangerous adventure.

When a test is coming up, get enough sleep, eat well, and exercise regularly, since the brain and hands that are going to work on that exam need to be in good shape. Don't keep cramming the night before and the morning of an exam. Just do a quick review to refresh your memory. Eat your normal breakfast, and think positive!

Right before the test, stay away from huddles with your classmates. Their information or misinformation will just be confusing, and their nervousness might be catching.

Laughter, though, can work wonders for both

physical and psychological states. So if you do talk with your fellow testers, keep it light and joking.

Take a deep breath as you take your seat, smile at someone, and make yourself comfortable.

Oh—one more testwise tip: Follow up. The testwise know that if they do badly on a quiz or exam, they should go to the teacher and review the problems they had with the test. Their grade might not go up this time, but they've at least made a good impression. Even if you want to protest what you feel is an unfair test or an inaccurate grade, when you do so politely, you will show that you are sincere about the importance of the course.

Tests to Test

CHAPTER 7

REAL TESTS TO TRY OUT

PRACTICE, PRACTICE, PRACTICE!

All test coaches—whether in print, in class, or online—say that the best way to do better on tests is to practice, practice, practice. You have your chance in this section. You'll find a lot of different kinds of tests and get a chance to put that preview . . . view . . . review system to work on all of them. Use that format and see how it works—with specialized tips—for each kind of test.

Remember—quizzes, exams, and standardized tests are all made up of one or a combination of these types of questions: multiple choice, true-false, fill-in-the-blanks, matching, essay, and computation. The content may vary—there may be number topics for word tests, or word problems for math tests. Some tests may require reading comprehension, or analogies between words, or comparisons of numbers. But the formats stay the same.

And the approach to doing your best on tests is the same no matter what: preview . . . view . . . review.

Now, apply the three steps of the system as you work these practice tests. Take out a pencil and a piece of paper. Look over each example, check the tips at the end of each type, then go back and use the tips to work the tests.

SHORT-ANSWER TESTS

Short-answer tests can take these forms:

MATCHING

Match the phrases in column B with the words from column A that best fit the meaning.

A	B
quiz	a useful attitude for test taking
practice	test that can mean as much as a big one
relaxed	preparation that begins the first school day
study	score that often matters too much
grade	one of the best ways to prepare for exam

TRUE-FALSE

Write T for true, F for false.

1. Good grades on a test show that you are smart. ____

2. Clues to the answer are never given in the question. ____

3. Test takers can expect true-false answers to follow a regular pattern, such as T F F T F. ____

4. The true-false part of a test is always counted as the least important. ____

5. Tests never scare some people. ____

6. This book guarantees you an A on every test. ____

7. Nobody feels that tests are fair. ____

FILL-IN-THE-BLANK

1. You are probably reading this book because you are _____ about taking tests.

2. Students who know how to take tests are called _____.

3. The best pattern to follow for studying and test taking is preview . . . _____ . . . review.

4. Checking the spelling is part of the _____ stage.

5. Outlining an essay is part of the _____ stage.

6. Allotting time is part of the _____ stage.

MULTIPLE CHOICE

Multiple-choice tests take some of these different forms:

1. Some good ways to prepare for a test are:
   - (a) Do homework daily.
   - (b) Practice.
   - (c) Ask a lot of questions.
   - (d) All of the above.

2. Circle the right word choice: It's *never/always* a good idea to ask questions about a test in advance.

3. Cross out the wrong word choice:
   A testwise person reads the questions *before/after* reading the test essay or homework chapter.

4. Write in the correct word:
   Multiple-choice questions are ____ scored with the same weight as other types of questions.
   - (a) never
   - (b) always
   - (c) sometimes
   - (d) all of the above

5. Circle the letter marking the correct word:
   When working a multiple-choice question, you should ____ the possible answers first.
   - (a) read
   - (b) mark
   - (c) ignore
   - (d) none of the above

ANALOGIES

Analogies are comparisons that are written to be read as "Blank is to blank as what is to what?"

1. Testwise:tests (Testwise is to tests as what is to what?)
   - (a) smart:gardening
   - (b) athletic:sports
   - (c) wise:religion

2. Short answers:exams
   - (a) trees:forest
   - (b) all:nothing
   - (c) question:answer

The following are some special tips when answering short-answer questions:

- Always read each instruction! (Did you do each item in the multiple-choice section according to the directions?)
- Always skim through the question first to see if you can answer it on your own, then find an option from among the multiple-choice selections that most nearly matches that idea.
- If you don't immediately know an answer, eliminate the options that you know cannot be right. In multiple-choice question 5, it's easy to see that option D cannot be right, so you are left with only three from which to choose.
- Once you have narrowed the choices to two, you are fairly safe in guessing, *unless* the test is one in which wrong answers are deducted from

right ones. In analogy 1, for instance, you know that "testwise" and "smart" aren't equal and that "gardening" has nothing to do with any of the items. So you have only two possibilities left to choose from.

- Look for clues in grammar and sense. In multiple-choice question 1, the grammar tells you there is more than one right answer. The only possible correct answer then is answer D.
- If necessary, work backward: Try each of the answers and see which one fits best. By using this system, you would find that D can't be the right answer for multiple-choice question 4.
- Remember that you are looking for the best answer from among your choices. You may be able to think up a "righter" answer, but you have only a limited selection of choices.

The following are some special tips when answering true-false questions:

- Look carefully at the qualifying words: Absolute words usually point to a "false," since few facts are absolute. In item 2, for instance, the word "never" makes the statement false. But the rule itself is not absolute: Item 5 is true despite its "never" because of that "some."

- Does the statement have any false parts? Item 6 begins as a true statement, but it is false because of its second half.

- Do *not* look for patterns. Teachers work hard to avoid patterns, and if there's a regular one, it's probably accidental, so don't take the chance. You *can* generally figure that the "true"s and "false"s will be about evenly balanced, however (with a tendency for more "true"s, if anything), so if the answers you've marked are heavily one or the other, you have a chance of being right if you fill in your blanks with the opposite answer.

- Unless you've been told not to, guess at answers that you aren't sure of. If you are penalized for wrong answers, don't guess. Since you have only two possibilities in a true-false test, you have a 50–50 chance of being right, so guessing here is safer than in other forms of tests.

PROBLEM-SOLVING TESTS

Problem-solving tests usually look like this:

1. What is the next number in this sequence?
1/10, 2/10, 3/10, 4/10, _____.

2. 4 + 9 = ____

        (a) 49

        (b) 13

        (c) 12

        (d) 94

3. 8 - 4 = ____

        (a) 5

        (b) 3

        (c) 4

        (d) 6

4. Which of the following is the opposite of 9 - 5 = 4?

        (a) 4 + 5 = 9

        (b) 5 - 4 = 1

        (c) 9 + 5 = 14

        (d) 9 + 4 = 13

The following are some special tips when answering problem-solving questions:

- Read the problem carefully to be sure you know what it is asking. If you are asked to find the sum, don't multiply!
- Reread the problem to get the facts you need for your work. Write them down and start to work the problem.
- On multiple-choice problems, make a rough estimate first and see if any of your options come close. Check your answer by working backward.

Watch for careless errors! You might feel that a long series of equations is a snap, but if in the middle of the problem you add when you should subtract, you will get the wrong answer.

ESSAY QUESTIONS

There are two types of essay questions.

Short essay questions are like these:

LISTS TO DEFINE OR IDENTIFY

Define the following words:

> 1. test
> 2. grade
> 3. review
> 4. preview
> 5. standardized

FILL-INS

Fill in the blanks with the best words or phrases:

1. The three stages for studying, _____, and test taking are preview, _____, _____.
2. Looking at the questions at the back of a textbook chapter is part of the _____ stage of a _____ assignment, because _____.

Long essay questions require both knowledge and an ability to organize that knowledge, as in these:

1. The test begins when you sit down and ends when you leave the room. Explain why or why not.

   _____

   _____

   _____

2. Outline the best procedure for studying and for taking tests. _____

   _____

   _____

3. Compare and contrast the difference between the way you take tests and the way the testwise student does. _____

   _____

   _____

4. Explain why you are reading this book. _____

   _____

   _____

   _____

The following are some tips on answering essay questions:

Essay questions are those that you answer from scratch—that is, you don't have any clues to build on. But there are tips to follow, for both short and long essay questions.

- If you have a choice among several questions to answer, read through all of them quickly to decide which to select.

- Then read the questions you choose carefully, looking for the key words that will tell you what is wanted in your essay. (In item 2, the key word is "outline.") Be sure you understand what the common key words mean. You will find a list of definitions, with examples, on pages 85–90.
- Budget your time: How many questions do you have to answer, and how long do you have for doing them? The sample test has five questions. A typical class hour is fifty minutes, which means that if you are instructed to answer all five questions, you would have ten minutes for each. You might know more about some questions than about others and so will need time to write more. The ones that are harder will take added thinking time, though, so it balances out. You also should allow some time for organizing your thoughts. A good way to get your thoughts organized is to pretend that you are the teacher, standing before the class and ticking off on your fingers the most important points.
- Jot down all of your ideas quickly and arrange them in a rough outline form. It would be a good idea to do this for all of the questions before you start to answer any of them fully, for two reasons: This really starts your mind working on

all the responses, and you will always have something down on paper even if time runs out.

• Plan to write as though you were the teacher, or as though you were trying to teach something to another person, rather than to show off all that you know. This approach gives you two advantages: It will make your answer more forceful and convincing, since you are, in effect, playing the role of the person with the knowledge; and, if you use your own teacher as a model, it will likely produce the kind of answer that your teacher might like best. (On question 2, for example, you would do well to answer according to the advice given in this book, whether you think it is "best" or not.)

• Try to compose a beginning, a middle, and an end. At the very least, your lead should be a topic sentence taken from the question. The lead for number 3 might be "There are many differences between the way I take tests and the way a testwise student does." Close with at least a short summary, for example, "To summarize, it is far better to be testwise."

• Give as many appropriate details as possible. Teachers have point scores in mind for each question and add up the number of points you include in each answer. In item 4, for instance, just saying "Because I had to" would not count for much.

- When you are not sure about a fact, qualify it with words like "often," "sometimes," "approximately," and so forth.
- Use the best grammar and spelling you can, and write clearly!
- If you run short of time, note that fact on your paper and finish your essay in quick outline form.
- However you manage it, always write *something*!
- Finally, even when time is short, always go back over your paper quickly.

KEY WORDS USED IN ESSAY QUESTIONS

Here is a list of the key words that you are likely to encounter in an essay test, along with sample questions and ways to approach answering each type of question. Each approach indicates a way to *begin* to answer this sort of question.

Analyze:	Break down a whole into the parts that make it up.
Sample question:	Analyze the characteristics that make dogs valuable to humans.
Sample approach:	Dogs are trainable for a variety of purposes. They display loyalty, affection, and dependency.

Compare: Find similarities and differences between two or more items, stressing similarities.

Sample question: Compare dogs with cats.

Sample approach: Both are four-legged mammals, and both are domesticated breeds of wild animals now commonly found as house pets.

Contrast: Examine associated items with an eye toward explaining differences.

Sample question: Contrast dogs with cats.

Sample approach: Dogs are found in a wider range of sizes than cats; dogs bark and cats meow.

Criticize: Express your judgment about the topic presented. Back up your opinion with analysis and explanation.

Sample question: Criticize dogs as pets.

Sample approach: Dogs can be messy and inconvenient because they are difficult to housebreak and require daily feeding and exercise.

Define: Give brief, clear meanings for words or concepts.

Sample question: Define "dog."

Sample approach: One of the earliest known domesticated animals, a descendant of

wolves tamed far back in prehistoric times.

Describe: Discuss the topic in accurate and
fine detail; give facts, not opinions.

Sample question: Describe the Cheshire cat.

Sample approach: The Cheshire cat looked like many
other cats when it was visible,
with four legs, soft fur, whiskers,
and a tail, but it could grow invis-
ible and, in the process, sometimes
all that could be seen was its head
or a wide, grinning smile.

Diagram: Make a drawing and label it.

Sample question: Diagram a cat.

Sample approach:

Discuss: Present background, significance,
and pros and cons. Back up each
statement with as much detail as
possible.

Sample question: Discuss the human domestication
of wild animals.

Sample approach: When humans tamed animals for
their own use, during prehistoric
times, they were able for the
first time to rely for food on sources
other than hunting or foraging.

Enumerate:	Make a list of topics or items. Focus on what, where, who, and/or when.
Sample question:	Enumerate the types of domesticated animals.
Sample approach:	dog, cat, sheep, cow, horse, pig.
Evaluate:	Rate or weight the significance of the topic and come to a conclusion.
Sample question:	Evaluate the human tendency of keeping pets.
Sample approach:	Psychologists find that pets can be of benefit to people, especially those who are lonely.
Explain:	Answer the "how" and "why" questions about a given topic. Interpret the facts you present and give causes for them.
Sample question:	Explain the affinity between people and pets.
Sample approach:	People need attachments and a feeling of worth. Pets offer both.
Illustrate:	Explain a concept or topic with a drawing, a graph, a diagram, or specific written examples.
Sample question:	Illustrate the people-pet connection in popular culture.
Sample approach:	We see the connection in such

comic strips as "Peanuts," "Garfield," and "Little Orphan Annie," where the animals have at least as much importance as the people.

Outline: Organize your answer in such a way that the subtopics or backup information are listed under main-topic heads.

Sample question: In outline form, describe a cat.
Sample approach: 1. Biological
        (a)
        (b)
        (c)

      2. Historic
        (a)
        (b)
        (c)

      3. Cultural
        (a)
        (b)
        (c)

Relate: Show the connections or associations between or among the topics given.

Sample question: Relate the needs of humans to the needs of domesticated animals.
Sample approach: Domesticated animals, whether

dogs, cows, cats, or pigs, need care and feeding, and people need the animals for a variety of purposes. To satisfy both needs, people care for animals.

Review: Enumerate, with some discussion, the major points of the topic presented—an examination that provides more detail than a list but less analysis than an evaluation.

Sample question: Review the similarities and differences between cats and dogs.

Sample approach: Cats and dogs are both domesticated animals having four legs, two ears, and a tail, but the two species have significant differences.

Essay, math, short-answer—no matter what form a test takes, the system is the same: preview . . . view . . . review.

And now that you see how simple any kind of test is, you will have no trouble with even the biggest, scariest, most important-looking test you'll face. Why? Because it is made up of most or all of the sections you just found out were so easy.

Prove it for yourself in the next chapter.

CHAPTER 8

THE REAL *BIG* TESTS— STANDARDIZED TESTS

WHEN YOU WERE FOUR, YOU MIGHT have taken a standardized aptitude test to get into a really good nursery school. In first grade you might have taken standardized achievement tests as practice for the "real thing" in second grade. And you've probably taken some type of standardized achievement test each year since then.

Companies that create tests try to make them interesting, attractive, and nonscary, but no matter what the format, they are usually presented as "big deals."

These are the tests that still frighten everyone—parents and teachers as well as students—in part because they seem powerful and mysterious. To make them easier to deal with, let's first clear away some of the mystery and myth.

The very name and form of these tests somehow make them seem perfect and all-important. Teachers and parents make a big deal out of them because they *do* matter both to you and to your school, but they're no different in content from other tests.

WHAT YOU NEED TO KNOW

Some of the words used in relation to testing are so complicated and scientific-sounding that they're scary. Here are some you'll likely run into. Once you know what they mean, they're easier to deal with.

Aptitude test: A test used to predict a student's future performance.

Achievement test: A test that measures knowledge, usually linked to a specific subject or course.

Computerized adaptive testing: Computerized testing that adjusts the difficulty of the test to the test taker's skill.

Criterion-referenced: A score derived by comparing a student's performance to a specific standard.

Grade equivalent score: A student's standing in test results stated in terms of school grade.

Multiple-choice question: A question that requires students to select an answer from a list of answers.

Norm-referenced: A score that compares a student's test result to that of a designated, or "norm," group.

Percentile rank: A comparison of one student's score with the scores of those of the norm group.

Portfolios: Collections of a student's work gathered over a period of time, designed as a record of achievement.

Reliability: A description of how consistent test scores will be from test to test.

Standardized test: A test that is administered and scored under the same conditions for all students taking that test.

PARENTS

Tests are often a big source of tension in families. It's good to take these tests seriously, but sometimes parents add to the tension rather than help you relax.

Parents may apply pressure in ways both obvious and not so obvious. Parents who insist that kids do well in school may punish them for a poor performance, so even a minor test becomes a much bigger deal.

You can check out parental attitudes by having

them read through this book. Or, maybe by sharing the information about standardized tests from the next section, you can help them relax.

Parents do have a part to play, however. If you have a parent who can *help* you study, quiz you on your notes, and the like, great! And if you have the kind of parent who gets really involved with your schoolwork, he or she can be useful in getting all the information possible about tests and testing that students often can't get hold of. (If you know ahead of time what kinds of tests you'll be taking when—and even the kinds of things that each type of test might cover—you're likely to feel more confident about them.)

Here's another area where parents can be of practical help. During teachers' meetings and parents' nights, as well as from the PTA, a parent can find out what testing schedule is planned for a given year. That way, you'll have an idea of what to get ready for, whether your teachers give you advance notice or not. Parents also have an easier time getting information about how the test scores will be used.

Parents can find out if test help is available at your school—and if not, they can work to get practice sessions established.

Other important questions they can get answered more easily are:

- What specific areas are being measured in tests?
- Will the material be covered ahead of time?
- How is the school performing as a whole on tests like these?

There are ways that parents can help their children with standardized tests. It's a matter of finding a way that's comfortable for you.

WHAT *ARE* STANDARDIZED TESTS, ANYWAY?

A test is "standardized" when the same questions, the same instructions, and the same formats are presented to groups of students around the world at virtually the same times of the school year and their school careers. Then the tests are scored or graded by a standardized process designed to remove the personal element and be more objective.

That's all!

If you are in grade four or above, you are taking standardized tests that:

- measure your progress in terms of what others

at your grade level have achieved, or against some standard of learning

- determine your placement in some subject area or in your upcoming level of school
- evaluate how good a job your school or school system is doing.

Yes, the "big" standardized tests can affect your life now and later—but they don't have to be frightening. The most important thing to remember about them is that they are made up of the same types of questions as all those classroom quizzes and tests—and the same three-step test-taking process applies. If you follow all the tips you've read in this book so far, when you take a standardized test, you will be able to handle that test calmly and successfully.

WHEN YOU GET TO THE TEST

When taking standardized tests, handling the nitty-gritty details can be as important as grasping the content of the exam.

Part of that nitty-gritty has to do with what you can expect when you walk into the testing room. If you are taking a standardized test such as the ISSEE, the SSAT, or others that are not required by the school you currently attend, you can expect to enter a large, bright room and be seated at a desk or desk chair well separated from your neighboring test taker, who is likely to be a stranger. Supervisors—or "proctors" or "monitors" (about one for every thirty test takers)—will be on hand to police the test.

Even if you are taking "simply" a school-required test, you should expect a similar-looking testing site. You may not see total strangers in the room, but you probably will see teachers who are not regularly in your classroom, since most schools assign alternate teachers to monitor tests.

So, you're in a strange room, or a room with strangers, and you're all hyped up for "The Test." The first thing you're asked to fill out has nothing to do with the test material. It will be a detailed personal questionnaire to make sure that the test taker is really who he or she claims to be. (Wouldn't it be great to have your genius cousin take your exam!) These questionnaires also provide the test publishers and the educational system with statistics about long-term trends. And while you're dealing with them, you'll probably find that you're also getting geared up to work with the "real stuff."

DEALING WITH DIRECTIONS

Once everyone has finished filling out the questionnaires, you'll be told how to proceed with the test. The directions will, of course, vary with each type of test, but you can expect to see a set of instructions that will cover the following points:

- An introduction to the overall exam: how many sections it contains, what they are, how much time is allotted to each one, and whether or not you can work on more than one section at once (in most cases, this is *not* permitted).
- Step-by-step procedures for answering the questions: how you go about deciding on an answer, and how you mark your choice—whether to write in the question booklet or on a separate answer sheet, whether to use a pencil (your own or a special one) or pen, and whether you can "scratch" on the booklet or a separate paper.
- Suggestions on how to go about working the test: Will wrong answers lose you points? Should you guess, or not?
- Each section of the test will have its own set of instructions, but you will not be able to read those until the supervisor tells you that you may.

- For some standardized tests, you will hear, rather than read, the instructions. All of them provide some spoken directions (such as what to do if you have a problem or a question, and when to begin and end). These are standardized, too, so that every test supervisor around the country is reading exactly the same thing.

TAKING THE TEST

OK, you know what to do, your pencil is poised, you've taken a deep breath to relax, and you're about to begin. Now what?

- Keep in mind that many grade-school-level tests are made to look *very* "friendly"—like workbooks. But they *are* tests, so take them seriously!
- Remember that your time allotment, your accuracy, and your attention to detail are more important for these exams, which will be scored by stencils or machines, than for a classroom test graded by a familiar teacher, so listen to the instructions and read the written directions very carefully. If you have any questions, ask them!
- Do not make any mark on the test paper other than your intended answer. On tests that are scored electronically, you risk confusing the

scoring if you make marks on anything but whatever scratch paper is provided. On hand-scored exams, the grader may not know which mark you meant. When you have made a mistake, or change your mind, erase completely. On multiple-choice questions, mark only one box—otherwise, the answer will count as wrong.

- Keep your question book and any separate answer sheet close to each other so that reading and marking are both convenient. And be sure to fill in the proper row! If your answers are right but accidentally marked in the wrong row, you may fail the entire test.

You will be better able to cope with any standardized tests when you realize that they are little different from any of the other tests you take week in and week out. So handle them by the same procedure: preview . . . view . . . review.

- Quickly read through the entire section you will be working on. Roughly allocate your time, and first answer the questions that are easiest. Rather than waste time working on one you're unsure of, mark the ones you know. However, avoid picking the most obvious answer automatically. Most items have two choices that "look good," but only one that is right.

- Then go back and work on the harder ones. Even if you are working on a test that penalizes you for guessing, you have several methods for making a well-educated guess, so don't panic or despair. Make sure that you have read the question accurately. Eliminate choices that you know are impossible. Look for clues within the question or problem itself. Try rewording the question or problem in a way that makes sense to you. Compare it with similar questions or problems that you were able to answer. If you're torn between two answers, go with the one that you think the testers are more likely to be looking for—the more general one, for instance. If you truly think that the question contains an ambiguity that makes more than one answer seem correct, raise your hand and ask about it.

- When the time you set aside for rechecking comes, go back and recheck! Review your answers and make sure you've marked the boxes accurately. Erase all errors *fully*. Even if you are allowed to leave the testing room whenever you are ready, use all of your time. Wise test takers know that there is always something more they can do on an exam.

TEST SAMPLES

The more familiar you are with what the tests are actually like, the better you'll do. So here are some examples of the kinds of standardized tests that you are likely to encounter. Get comfortable with them. See how similar they are to all the "smaller" tests you've been doing throughout this book.

For instance: Pages you might see if you were going to take a CAT, a MAT, a Stanford, or a CTBS might look like some of the examples on the following pages.

Some standardized tests look like this list of problems.

Computation
Multiplying

At the bottom of the page, fill in the circle for the correct answer in the following multiplication problems. Fill in the circle for *None of these* if the answer is not given.

DO THIS Multiply each set of numbers. Work the problems on this sheet. Circle the answer, then compare it with the choices given. Mark your answer code below.

Sample X

$\begin{array}{r} 8 \\ \times 3 \\ \hline \end{array}$

A 24
B 5
C 11
D 83
E None of these

HOW TO DO IT! The correct answer is (A). (B) would be the answer if you were asked to subtract and (C) if you added; (D) is wrong. Don't forget to mark answer X below.

─────── STOP

1

$49 \times 9 = \underline{\hspace{1cm}}$

A 58
B 450
C 499
D 441
E None of these

4

$\begin{array}{r} \$15.00 \\ \times \ \ 4.10 \\ \hline \end{array}$

F $6.15
G $61.50
H $60.10
J $60.00
K None of these

2

$\begin{array}{r} 14 \\ \times 39 \\ \hline \end{array}$

F 394
G 53
H 615
J 546
K None of these

5

$12 \times 32 \times 7 = \underline{\hspace{1cm}}$

A 2688
B 384
C 224
D 41
E None of these

3

$\frac{1}{3} \times \frac{2}{3} = \underline{\hspace{1cm}}$

A ⅓
B ⅚
C ⅝
D ½
E None of these

6

$0.4 \times 0.8 = \underline{\hspace{1cm}}$

F 320
G 0.12
H 0.32
J 4.8
K None of these

─────── STOP

Answers

X Ⓐ Ⓑ Ⓒ Ⓓ Ⓔ   2 Ⓕ Ⓖ Ⓗ Ⓙ Ⓚ   4 Ⓕ Ⓖ Ⓗ Ⓙ Ⓚ   6 Ⓕ Ⓖ Ⓗ Ⓙ Ⓚ
1 Ⓐ Ⓑ Ⓒ Ⓓ Ⓔ   3 Ⓐ Ⓑ Ⓒ Ⓓ Ⓔ   5 Ⓐ Ⓑ Ⓒ Ⓓ Ⓔ

Some look more like this—a friendly workbook.

Kay would really like to see the world, but she's simplified that goal. This has helped her visit her aunt in Minnesota because she *wants to* get away, she *has to* go somewhere cheap, and she *ought to* visit her aunt.

So she begins to aim toward her *long-range goal* of a trip to Minnesota.

When will she go? She wants to go in August because it's very hot at home then and cooler in Minnesota. Also, it will give her a vacation between her summer job and her return to school. Besides, her aunt will be away for part of that month, so Kay can stay at her aunt's house and use her car for part of the vacation, and that will save money while still allowing her to visit with her aunt.

August is five months away, so now Kay has a medium-range goal to aim for: She will need X dollars for the trip. Kay has Y dollars in her savings account that she won't be using for other things, so her short-range goal is to collect the rest of the money. That means Kay needs to aim toward a high-paying summer job.

1. What is the first action Kay takes toward her travel goal?_____

_____

_____

_____

2. Why does Kay want to go to Minnesota?

_____

_____

_____

_____

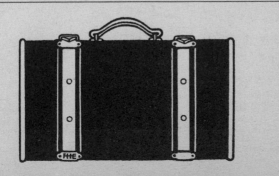

Some tests use no words at all.

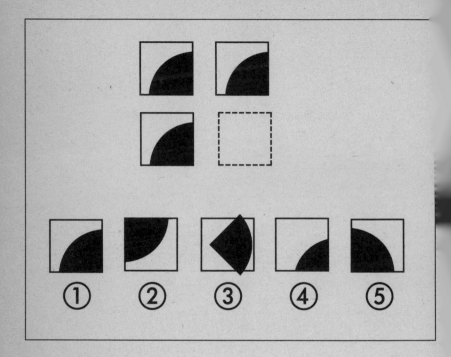

But they are all tests, and all need to be taken seriously.

Some standardized tests ask you to mark your answers on a separate sheet of paper, like the answer sheet on the next page. Be careful!

A	B	C	D	A	B	C	D	A	B	C	D	A	B	C	D
0	0	0	0	0	0	0	0	0	0	0	0	0	0	0	0
0	0	0	0	0	0	0	0	0	0	0	0	0	0	0	0
0	0	0	0	0	0	0	0	0	0	0	0	0	0	0	0
0	0	0	0	0	0	0	0	0	0	0	0	0	0	0	0
0	0	0	0	0	0	0	0	0	0	0	0	0	0	0	0
0	0	0	0	0	0	0	0	0	0	0	0	0	0	0	0
0	0	0	0	0	0	0	0	0	0	0	0	0	0	0	0
0	0	0	0	0	0	0	0	0	0	0	0	0	0	0	0
0	0	0	0	0	0	0	0	0	0	0	0	0	0	0	0
0	0	0	0	0	0	0	0	0	0	0	0	0	0	0	0
0	0	0	0	0	0	0	0	0	0	0	0	0	0	0	0
0	0	0	0	0	0	0	0	0	0	0	0	0	0	0	0
0	0	0	0	0	0	0	0	0	0	0	0	0	0	0	0
0	0	0	0	0	0	0	0	0	0	0	0	0	0	0	0
0	0	0	0	0	0	0	0	0	0	0	0	0	0	0	0
0	0	0	0	0	0	0	0	0	0	0	0	0	0	0	0
0	0	0	0	0	0	0	0	0	0	0	0	0	0	0	0
0	0	0	0	0	0	0	0	0	0	0	0	0	0	0	0
0	0	0	0	0	0	0	0	0	0	0	0	0	0	0	0
0	0	0	0	0	0	0	0	0	0	0	0	0	0	0	0
0	0	0	0	0	0	0	0	0	0	0	0	0	0	0	0
0	0	0	0	0	0	0	0	0	0	0	0	0	0	0	0
0	0	0	0	0	0	0	0	0	0	0	0	0	0	0	0
0	0	0	0	0	0	0	0	0	0	0	0	0	0	0	0
0	0	0	0	0	0	0	0	0	0	0	0	0	0	0	0
0	0	0	0	0	0	0	0	0	0	0	0	0	0	0	0
0	0	0	0	0	0	0	0	0	0	0	0	0	0	0	0
0	0	0	0	0	0	0	0	0	0	0	0	0	0	0	0

Some ask you to mark or write right on the page. The instructions will tell you what to do!

LISTENING SKILLS

Instructions

A paragraph will be read aloud. Listen carefully to it. Take notes if you like. Then listen to the questions. Pick the best answer and mark the letter next to it on the answer sheet.

Jessie has set her alarm fifteen minutes early because Tuesday's her day to take her brother Nathan to school, and, since she's starting her diet today, she has to make a salad for herself for lunch. She's talked her friends into having a picnic lunch because if she spends too much money on food, she won't be able to buy her friend Gary a birthday present. She's planning to get him something at the shopping center when she goes for groceries. If she gets it now, she'll know how much money she has left over for the week—maybe enough to buy some new clothes for the party.

Jessie is hoping to have enough money
     (A) for lunch.
     (B) for groceries.
     (C) for a present.
     (D) for a diet.

Jessie set her alarm early
     (A) because she wanted extra sleep.
     (B) because it was Wednesday.
     (C) because she had to take her brother to school.
     (D) because Nathan told her to.

Look at the test samples that follow. See how some of the formats and answering systems may seem alike but are really different.

Reading Matching

| DO THIS | Look at the picture carefully. Read each word and decide if it tells about something in the picture. Then fill in the circle under the word that matches. |

Mark the words that are found in this picture:

1. glass   girl   grill
   O   O   O
2. brush   brass   broom
   O   O   O

Mark the words that are found in this picture:

3. swing   sun   swim
   O   O   O
4. shorts   shoes ship
   O   O   O

Darken the circle for the correct answer. If the correct answer is not given, darken the circle for *None of these*.

1. This is Bill and his ice-cream cone. His mother gave him $2.00 for ice cream. The cone cost $1.25. How much money does Bill have left?

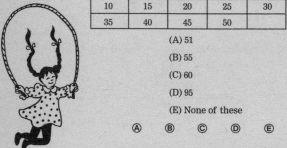

      (A) $1.00

      (B) $.75

      (C) $1.75

      (D) $3.25

      (E) None of these

    Ⓐ   Ⓑ   ©   Ⓓ   Ⓔ

2. Each time Alisha practices, she can jump five more times than last without a mistake. Here is her chart. How many times will she jump next?

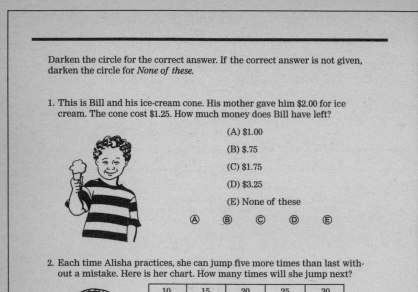

10	15	20	25	30
35	40	45	50	

      (A) 51

      (B) 55

      (C) 60

      (D) 95

      (E) None of these

    Ⓐ   Ⓑ   ©   Ⓓ   Ⓔ

3. Every day Tim's mom reads 10 pages of this book. The book has 44 pages. She has been reading for two days. How many pages are left to read?

      (A) 20

      (B) 24

      (C) 10

      (D) 2

      (E) None of these

    Ⓐ   Ⓑ   ©   Ⓓ   Ⓔ

Think About It

Directions: Fill in the circle for the correct answer.

> **THINK ABOUT IT** Read the question. Study the picture. Find the information you need to pick the right answer from the choices.

Sample X

Mary has been jogging a little more each day. This chart shows her training pattern. What number goes in the empty box?

	Monday	Wednesday	Friday
week 1	2 mi.	2.25 mi.	2.5 mi.
week 2		3 mi.	3.25 mi.

(A) 2.50 mi.
(B) 3 mi.
(C) 2.75 mi.
(D) None of these

1. Jessie can walk a block in two minutes. If Jessie has to stop at the store on the way to school, how much longer will she take to get there?

store

1.5 blocks

1 block

Jessie's house

2 blocks

school

(A) 2.5 minutes
(B) 1 minute
(C) 4 minutes
(D) None of these

2. Sal is allowed to watch 1 ½ hours of TV today. His favorite show lasts ½ hour. How much more TV can he watch?

(A) 1 1-hour show
(B) 2 ½-hour shows
(C) 1 1 ½-hour show
(D) A and B

Answers

X ⒶⒷⒸⒹ   2 ⒶⒷⒸⒹ

1 ⒶⒷⒸⒹ

Darken the circle for the correct answer.

1. Which bird is flying?

      (A)   (B)   (C)   (D)

A B C D
○ ○ ○ ○

2. Which striped animal has a name beginning with *T*? Circle it.

3. Which has horns?

  A B
  ○ ○

4. Which has thorns?

  A B
  ○ ○

              (A)   (B)

How to Study

Directions: Fill in the circle for the correct answer.

THINK ABOUT IT	Read the question. Study the picture. Find the information you need to pick the right answer from the choices.

Sample X

Jake needs to know the history of flying. Where should he look?

(A) Dictionary
(B) Encyclopedia
(C) Plane geometry
(D) None of the above

1. Jerry needs to find some information. Where will he find today's sports scores?

(A) Newspaper
(B) TV
(C) Encyclopedia
(D) A and B

Answers

X Ⓐ Ⓑ Ⓒ Ⓓ

1 Ⓐ Ⓑ Ⓒ Ⓓ

Here's one last sample test to check out.

Mark the circle under the last letter of
the names of each of these animals.

A	K	B	Y
○	○	○	○

T	D	Y	G
○	○	○	○

u	w	c	o
○	○	○	○

b	F	h	d
○	○	○	○

Did you pay attention to the instructions that
asked for the *last* letter of the name?

CHAPTER 9

WHERE TO FIND MORE TESTS

IF SOME PRACTICE IS GOOD, MORE IS better. While it would be nice to have the actual tests to practice on, that's not possible, of course. But there are ways to get extra practice on standardized tests—the ones you'll be taking and ones *like* the ones you'll take.

Here are some ways to learn more about the tests—how to get ready for them and what they mean—before and after a test:

- Teachers can often get samples of the tests. However, they are limited as to when and how they can share them with students.

- You (or a parent) can get test catalogs and sample booklets from many big test companies. Write to them at the following addresses:

For the Stanfords:
Harcourt Brace Educational Measurement
555 Academy Street
San Antonio, TX 78204

For the Iowas:
Riverside Publishing
425 Spring Lake Drive
Itasca, IL 60143-2079

For practice tests and test-related materials:
Steck-Vaughn Company
4515 Seton Center Parkway
Austin, TX 78759

Most test publishing companies have toll-free phone numbers. You can find them by calling the 800–555–1212 information number and asking for the company by name.

The following test makers are online. Use "search" to find the best Web addresses.

The College Board
Consulting Psychologists Press
CTB McGraw-Hill
Educational Records Bureau

Educational Testing Service
Harcourt Brace Educational Measurement
The Psychological Corporation
Riverside Publishing Company

With a computer—either at home, at school, or at the library—you can go onto the World Wide Web and find test-practice material. Here are some good sites:

"ERIC" Test Locator
Provided by the U.S. Department of Education, this site contains an online, searchable database of test descriptions.
Web site: www.ERICacceric@inet.ed.gov

Educational Testing Service (ETS)
A major test publisher of such standardized tests as the PSAT. See the ETS section entitled Practice Test Questions.
Web site: www.ets.org

EDUTEST (International Educational Testing)
Offers tests for elementary school students, based on the standards for learning and achievement of the state of Virginia.
Web site: www.test.com

And what about test coaching? Experts disagree about the value of coaching, but some people think it's necessary. If you want to explore test-prep services, here's how to contact some of the big ones:

Educational Testing Service (ETS)
A wealth of descriptive information and practice test questions from a major test publisher of such standardized tests as the PSAT.
Web site: www.ets.org

Kaplan
Offers coverage of standardized tests and admissions procedures.
Web site: www.kaplan.com

The Princeton Review
A full-service preparatory service that offers information about testing companies, including phone numbers and test taking problems.
Web site: www.review.com

CHAPTER 10

IS IT OVER YET?

You may think that once a standardized test is handed in, your mission is complete. No, it's not!

Chapter 6 suggested going to your teacher to review the results of a classroom test. That kind of review is possible—and useful—with standardized tests, too.

When a test grade comes back that's not what you expected, whether it's a classroom test or a standardized one, you don't just have to accept the outcome. In fact, it's part of the learning experience to find out what you did wrong.

This is a point in the testing process when parents can come in very handy. Most kids don't want a parent storming into their class, making threats or whining. But parents can gain access to tests that students may not. In fact, most of the major test publishers provide teachers with printed information on how to explain test scores to parents.

So the first person a parent should go to is your classroom teacher. Even if they aren't disturbed by a score you might have received, just having a clear explanation of what all the odd numbers mean is worthwhile—"Stanine scores," "means and medians," "grade references," and similar phrases are a language that needs translating.

Also, test scorers do sometimes make mistakes, and scores can be challenged. This can be important as you work your way through your test-taking career, since the magic number on a test report sheet can make a difference in where you'll be placed in school.

In addition to the classroom teacher, the test publishers are also a resource for scoring information. Find out which publisher produced the test that concerns you, and refer to the previous chapter for contact information.

WHAT'S AHEAD FOR YOU?

A big question, especially for someone your age looking ahead to a long pathway of tests, is: What's ahead in testing? As you go through your school (and testing) career, you may encounter new kinds of tests that you may already be hearing about now.

There is ongoing discussion about relying less on standardized tests, but they will probably continue to count for a lot. Plans for a national standardized test that would be given to all students in the country are being discussed, but there is a lot of argument about this idea, too, so you may not actually have another exam added to your schedule during your school career.

Portfolios are now being used along with more formal test scores to measure a student's ability. Many educators think this technique of gathering all of a student's work samples is a valuable system. However, even if there's not the tension around it that there is around exams, you still need to take this measurement of your abilities and progress seriously.

Computerized testing is another hot phrase, but it will probably not come into common usage until all schools and libraries have good computers.

In any case, whenever you take a test, from whatever source, you can still look ahead to counting on the same test-taking process: preview . . . view . . . review.

WHAT DO YOU KNOW?

Stop! What's the last thing you do in any learning or testing process? Right—you *review*.

This book, like almost all books, has a built-in review system. Turn back to the table of contents. Go down it, entry by entry. For each entry, mentally review what was in that section or chapter. If you hit something that's a mystery, turn to the page and look it over again.

Now you're ready—and here's a handy way to remember how to do your best on *any* test:

Preview
Ahead of time

- Ask questions about the test and testing method.
- Practice if possible.
- Prepare mentally.
- Prepare physically.
- Prepare emotionally.

At test time

- Pay close attention to the instructions, both verbal and written.
- Do you have questions? Ask!

View

- Look over the whole test, if possible, to get your brain in gear.
- Do you have questions? Ask!
- Do the easiest test questions first.
- Go back to the harder questions.

Review

- Recheck those test questions you're unsure of.
- Do you have questions? Ask!
- Check all answers.
- Make sure the answers are in line with the instructions.
- Clean and correct marks.

INDEX

achievement tests, 10, 92
acronyms for memorization, 54
addresses for sample tests, 116–18
analogies. *See* word-analogy tests
aptitude tests, 10, 92
assignments, writing down of, 38
attitude of student, 36–38

behavior before the test, 68–69
blank paper, turning in of, 56
brainstorming, 60

classroom tests
  as about one-third of final grade, 9
  as guide to final test, 43
  importance of, 8–10
  review with teacher of, 43, 69, 119
coaching for standardized tests, 117–18
College Board, The, 116
comprehension tests, 14
computation tests, 14, 57
  partial answers for, 60
  your own practice for, 49
computerized adaptive testing, 92
computerized testing, 121

Consulting Psychologists Press, 116
cramming, 50–51, 68
criterion-referenced tests, 92
CTB McGraw-Hill, 116

definitions, memorization of, 53
definition tests, 81, 86–87
diagram tests, 87

easy or hard stuff first, 28–29, 34, 59–60, 100–101
Educational Records Bureau, 116
Educational Testing Service (ETS), 117, 118
EDUTEST, 117
"ERIC" Test Locator, 117
essay tests (essay questions)
  definition of, 14
  examples of, for practice, 81–82
  key words used in, 85–90
  partial answers for, 61
  practice for, 47–48
  preview of, 58
  short vs. long, 81
  time allotted for, 83, 85
  tips on, 82–85

fear of tests, 62–64
fill-in-the-blanks tests, 14

examples of, for practice, 75, 81

your own practice for, 49

final exam

  finding out subjects covered by, 43

  form of, 43–44

  studying for, 42–49

friends, doing practice exams with, 47

goals, 34

grade equivalent score, 92

grammar and punctuation tests, 56–57

grouping items for memorization, 53

guessing

  in short-answer tests, 77–78, 79

  in standardized tests, 101

Harcourt Brace Educational Measurement, 116, 117

hard or easy stuff first, 28–29, 34, 59–60, 100–101

hearing, learning by, 35–36, 52

homework

  preview...view...review of, 32

  putting off until tomorrow, 34

initial words for memorization, 54

instructions for a test, 18–20, 27–28

review of, 29

short-answer tests, 77

standardized tests, 98–99

International Educational Testing, 117

Internet

  test makers' addresses on, 116–17

  test practice material on, 117

jingles for memorization, 54

Kaplan, 118

key words as help in memorization, 53

laughter before the test, 68–69

learning, three methods of, 35–36

matching tests, 14

  examples of, for practice, 74

melody for memorization, 54

memorization

  incentive for, 51

  techniques and tricks for, 52–54

memory, long-term vs. short-term, 50, 52

mental pictures, 52–53

middle sections of material, best starting with, 45

midterm exam, 42

multiple-choice questions on standardized tests, 93, 100

multiple-choice tests, 14
  examples of, for
    practice, 75–76

norm-referenced tests, 93
notes
  classroom, 38
  while reading, 39
  review of, 40, 46

outline questions, 89
out-loud recitation, 46
overlearning as
    necessary, 45

parents, standardized
    tests and, 93–95, 120
partial answers in tests,
    60–61
percentile rank, 93
perfectionism, 34–35
physical learning, 35–36, 52
portfolios, 93, 121
practice tests
  examples of, to try out,
    73–90
  made up by yourself,
    46–49
preview
  of book or chapter,
    38–39
  definition of, 12–13, 25
  of tests, 26–28, 42, 45,
    56–59, 122–23
preview...view...review,
    12–13, 16, 25–30, 122–23
  of final exam, 42, 45
  in reading, 38–41
  in studying for tests, 31–41
Princeton Review, The, 118

problem-solving tests
  examples of, for
    practice, 79–80
  tips for, 80–81
  your own practice for, 49
Psychological
  Corporation, The, 117
putting off until
    tomorrow, 34

quizzes. See classroom
  tests

reading-comprehension
  tests
  preview of, 58
  view of, 60
reading, preview...
  view...review in, 38–41
recitation out loud, 46
relaxation techniques, 55,
  64–68
reliability of tests, 93
review
  of book or chapter,
    39–40
  definition of, 13, 25
  in essay question, 90
  frequency of, as best, 41
  of standardized tests, 101
  of tests, 29–30, 61, 123
rhymes for memorization,
  54
rhythm for memorization,
  54
Riverside Publishing
  Company, 116, 117

sample tests, 102–14
  where to get, 115–17

seeing, learning by, 35–36, 52

sentence completion tests. *See* fill-in-the-blanks tests

short-answer tests
    examples of, for practice, 74–79
    tips for, 77–79
    your own practice for, 48–49

standardized tests, 91–114
    coaching for, 117–18
    definition of, 93
    fear of, 91–92
    future of, 121
    how to take, 99–101
    importance of, 10
    instructions for, 98–99
    purpose of, 95–96
    review of test scores of, 119–20
    samples of, 102–14
    testing sites for, 96–97
    types of, 92–93
    where to get samples of, 115–17

Steck-Vaughn Company, 116

study attitude, 36–38

studying
    for final exam, 42–49
    preview...view...review in, 31–41

study style, 32–36

tape recording, 46, 52, 54

teachers
    making a good impression on, 37

review of bad tests with, 43, 69, 119
    scaring of students by, 17
    standardized-test information for, 115, 120

teaching methods, classroom tests as indicator of quality of, 8

tension-relieving techniques, 55, 64–68

test-prep services, 118

testwise
    definition of, 13
    how to become, 16–21

textbook, marking of, 39

three-step system. *See* preview...view...review

time allotment
    for essay questions, 83, 85
    for standardized tests, 99
    for tests, 60–61

true-false tests, 14, 58
    examples of, for practice, 75
    tips for, 78–79
    your own practice for, 49

types of tests, 13–14, 46, 73–74

view
    of book or chapter, 39
    definition of, 12, 25
    of standardized tests, 99–101
    of tests, 28–29, 59–61, 123

word-analogy tests, 57
    examples of, for practice, 76–77

4713